THE ADVENTURES OF SERJEANT BENJAMIN MILLER,

During his service in the 4th Battalion, Royal Artillery, from 1796 to 1815.

With an Introduction by Miss M. R. Dacombe, M.A., and Miss B. J. H. Rowe, M.A., B.Litt.

———

Benjamin Miller was born on 2 April, 1776. He enlisted in the Royal Regiment of Artillery on 9 December, 1796, from which he received his discharge on 1 April, 1815, upon a pension of 1s. 6½d. a day.

The manuscript which is here set forth is the property of the great-grandson of the writer, Mr. Alfred G. Miller, of Worthing, through whose courtesy it is now published. It is contained in a book, with stiff paper cover, of 106 numbered, and a few un-numbered pages, the page measuring 8¼″ by 6¾″. The water-mark ' 1813 ' appears on some of the pages. On the inside of the cover is a *printed* account of evidence given in a trial in London, which terminated on 19 July, 1820.

The autobiography in its present form was therefore *certainly* not compiled before 1813, *possibly* not before 1820, although the cover, which appears to be ' home-made,' may have been added later the better to preserve the manuscript.

According to Benjamin's great-nephew, Mr. T. S. Miller, of Wimborne, Dorset, the actual diary, which forms the basis of the manuscript as it now stands, was at one time partially burnt. When the serjeant copied it out, adding extra details, he never filled up the gap caused by the fire, and this explains the silence during the period 1804 to 1808. So far as it has been possible to check them, Miller's dates and facts are, with one or two exceptions (*e.g.* the record for the months of May and June, 1801), extraordinarily accurate. In the printed text, the spelling throughout has been corrected, and, where necessary, modernised.

The following information has also been kindly furnished by Mr. T. S. Miller, whose father (who died in December, 1924) remembered Benjamin well:—

After his discharge in 1815, Benjamin returned to his native village, Melbury Osmond, near Yeovil, and settled there for the rest of his life. He and other old soldiers, drawing pensions, used to hire a cart and drive to Yeovil once a quarter to receive their money.

The Volunteers at Evershot used to invite Miller to their annual dinner, where he was an honoured guest because he could make a good speech. He died at Melbury Osmond on 3 February, 1865, aged 88, and was buried there on 10 February.

His wife, *née* Sarah Butcher, was born at Boughton, near Fareham in Kent, on 5 July, 1782, and was regarded as somewhat a stranger in the Dorset village. She spoke purer English than the villagers, and taught her children to do the same. She survived her husband and died on 16 February, 1873, aged 91, and was buried at Melbury Osmond. There are no headstones on their graves, which, it is to be regretted, cannot now be identified.

Benjamin's eldest grandson, also Benjamin, after serving his apprenticeship to a village cobbler, joined the Baptist Ministry, and was Minister at Cullompton, Devon, for 19 years. His youngest son is Mr. Alfred G. Miller, of Worthing, the owner of the " diary," and a coal merchant.

It is on record that Miller, at the time of his enlistment, was 5ft. 7 ins. in height, with fair complexion, dark eyes, and light hair, and that he was a ' leather-dresser ' by trade. (Public Record Office. W.O. 54/277 and 278.)

He enlisted for ' unlimited service.' The dates of his promotion to higher ranks are.—

Bombardier	...	8 October, 1804.
Corporal	...	1 February, 1809.
Serjeant	...	1 October, 1811.

Miller was entitled to the silver General Service medal with clasps for Egypt and Coruña. The grant of this medal to those who had served in the Peninsular and other wars, with clasps for ' Coruña ' (spelled ' Corunna ') and for other battles, was authorized by Horse Guards' General Order of 1 June, 1847.

Miller's medal was sold at auction in 1918 to a Mr. Weight, a dealer in medals, since dead, but its present resting-place is, unfortunately, not known.

Mention is made in the notice of his death—3 February, 1865—in a local newspaper that " he fought at the battle of Coruña, under Sir John Moore, for which he received a medal about 40 years after the event." Information has been furnished by the War Office to the effect that this medal, with clasp for " Corunna " only, was awarded and issued to Miller, but there is no record in the Medal Rolls of the clasp ' Egypt ' being awarded.

This is probably due to the fact that the clasp ' Egypt ' was not authorized until 1850—Horse Guards' General Order of 12 February, 1850, published in *The London Gazette* of the same date. There is no doubt, however, that Miller was fully entitled to the clasp ' Egypt.'

Miller was obviously above the average ability of the countrymen of his day. He learnt to read and write while he was page-boy at Madam Knight's (see text), and he had been well drilled in a knowledge of the Scriptures. As far as we know he never went to school, but while at Closworth he had greater opportunity of educating himself than had many village boys at that time.

His story from a soldier's point of view is most interesting—his conversation with the Roman priests in Minorca show him as an ardent

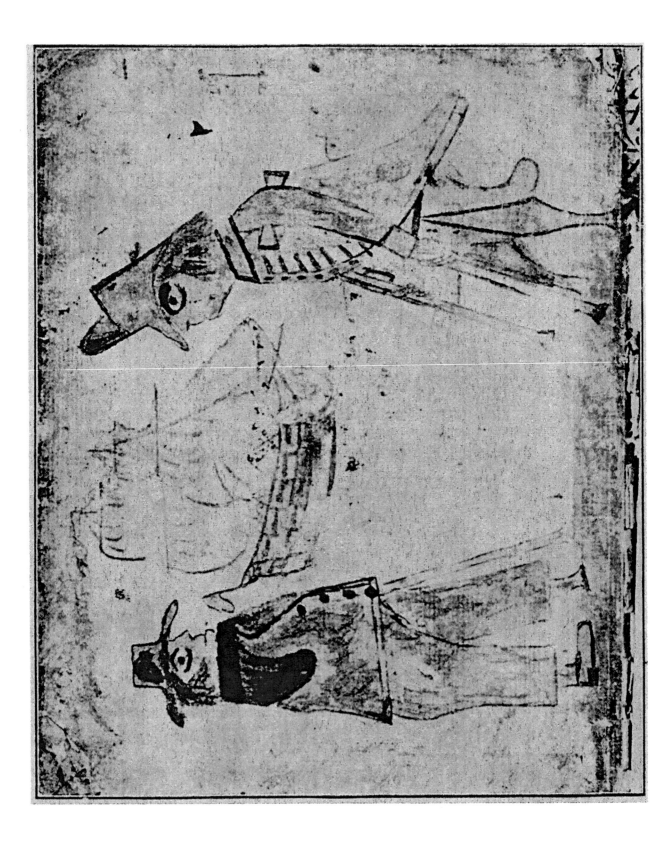

theologian, and the incident in Egypt when a " poor old grey-headed Frenchman," who had begged for mercy, was bayoneted, and our soldiers cried out " shame " shows that they held right-minded ideas and were not unkindly disposed to an enemy. There can be very few soldiers, too, who are able to record that Sir John Moore spoke to them on the day on which he was killed.

Miller was, certainly, a stout-hearted man, as is amply testified by his philosophic remark, on landing at Ramsgate in February, 1809, after the terrible experiences of the Coruña campaign and the voyage back to England. Although he was without money to buy food or drink, and with a 16 mile march before him, he merely remarks that " we were well used to such fare, and knew it would soon be over, so we thought nothing of it."

Miller was no " grouser," so let us all take our hats off to his memory and congratulate ourselves that he has left behind him this straightforward and very entertaining book.

The footnotes and all matter enclosed in square brackets have been added by Lieut.-Colonel J. H. Leslie.

The sketch, in sepia, facing this page, appears at the end of the MS., and, presumably, represents a soldier and a sailor of the period—*circa* 1815-20.

The drawing is crude, but the uniform dress is probably correct. The soldier, as will be seen, has lost both legs, and the sailor one, and the latter appears to have lost his right arm.

THE GENERAL SERVICE SILVER MEDAL.
(See Supplement to *The London Gazette*, of 1 June, 1847, page 2043.)

THE MANUSCRIPT.

Benjamin Miller, son of Benjamin and Catharine Miller, [was] born the 2nd Day of April, in the Year of our Lord 1776, at Melbury Osmond,* North-end County of Dorset.

My father went Substitute in the Dorset Militia [in] 1778, and went to Coxheath Camp‡ where my Mother, with me and my Brother, followed him.

In 1780 he left the Militia and returned to Melbury.

In 1782 my father went to Portsmouth, where my mother, with me, my brother & two sisters, followed him. He was employed in Portsmouth Dockyard. My Mother died at Portsmouth, on 12 May, 1789, and was buried at Kingston, Portsea, and left my father with six children. I was the oldest, not 13 years of age. I was so troubled at the death of my mother that I sat down when out one day by my self and prayed to God to take me along with my mother.

After the death of my mother we returned to Melbury, where we were almost starved to death. But I got a good place at Madam Knight's at Closworth§ and remained there 3 years, until the old Lady died. From thence I went back to Melbury and learnt to weave. But not being healthy at that business I bound my self to Mr. Penny, Gloving-master, at Yeovil, Somerset.** My wage being so very small, I could not live, and also being rather of a roving disposition I enlisted into the Royal Regiment of Artillery, with Serjeant Somerville at Yeovil, on 9 December, 1795.

1796.

Joined the Regiment at Woolwich with 15 other Recruits, 11 February, 1796. [He was mustered in March, 1796, in Captain J. G. Fraser's Detachment—*vide* Muster Rolls in P.R.O.] Went to drill; liked it very well, being well used.

Volunteered for Gibraltar and embarked in the *Pallas*, transport, from Woolwich Warren on 7 March. Next day was shifted from the *Pallas* to the *Grand*, transport, and sailed down the river Thames and joined a Convoy at the Downs. Left the Downs on 12 March and bore away for Spithead. Four of our convoy were taken by French Privateers before we got to Spithead.

Left Spithead on 2 April, my birthday. Could see the spot from the ship's deck (on shore at Portsmouth) where I had seen 8 birthdays, which brought my deceased mother strong on my memory. But we soon lost sight of it and Albion's chalky cliffs, together with a large fleet under convoy of the *Goliath*, 74, with our hearts full of glee, but little thinking it was for a 14 years cruise or of the danger and hardships we had to endure before our return.

3 [April]. Lost sight of old England. 4 [April]. Entered the Bay

* 6 miles due S. from Yeovil.   ‡ 3 miles S. from Maidstone, Kent.
§ 3½ miles due S. from Yeovil.
** Then, as now, a centre of the glove-making industry.

1796.

of Biscay, where we were becalmed 14 days, at which time the itch broke out in our ship; we were in a sad mess.

On 18 April sprang up a brisk gale and we made way. We saw two large hogs making towards our ship which made us ask if hogs were amphibious, but we soon found they were washed from another ship's deck. We got them on board by lashing a rope round a man's middle and letting him into the sea.

19 April. A signal was made for the convoy to separate and to steer to their different destinations (some to all parts of the globe).

20 April. Passed an English Squadron of frigates who told us to keep a good look out, for a French fleet was off Cadiz. We soon perceived 9 sail of men-of-war. Then the women began to sound their trumpets and the officers to conceal their money, for we expected we should all be taken prisoners. But to our great joy it proved to be Admiral [Robert Man] with 9 sail of British men of war actually watching for a French fleet. He put us out of fear by telling us he would see us safe into the Gut [i.e. the Straits. Ed.] of Gibraltar if we would wait a day or two.

So on 29 April entered the Gut and anchored in Gibraltar Bay, after dark.

At daylight next morning [30 April] we went on deck thinking to see a fine Town and Country, but were much surprised to find nothing but a tremendous rock reaching its craggy summit above the clouds and surrounded by the ocean. The town was not to be seen from the harbour.

2 May. We landed and I verily thought I was got into some enchanted land, to see wagon loads of oranges, and all other kind of fruits lying in heaps on the ground, and groups of savage Moors, more like wild beasts than human beings, sitting cross-legged on the ground selling it. Next we came to the Barracks, more like sheds they build in the fields of England for cattle in stormy weather and paved after the manner of a stable.

> Hard is the Soldier's lot
> that is transported to that barren Rock,
> To be tormented by bugs and fleas
> and do hard duty on pork and peas.

I went to the Hospital the same day we landed, but could get no sleep at night for fear of the scorpions and centipedes, which are very numerous in Gibraltar.

[Here he joined Captain John Bradbridge's Company, 4th Battalion, Royal Artillery, which had been stationed at Gibraltar since June, 1793. This Company is in 1928 represented by 14 Heavy Battery, R.A.]

After coming from the Hospital I had enough to do to gaze at the inhabitants which are from all nations under the sun; a greater contrast in features and manners is no where to be found, and any person that wishes to see the dress and customs of all the world, let him go to Gibraltar.

The rock is 8 miles in circumference and 3 miles in length, surrounded by water except a narrow isthmus from it to Spain.

1796.

Seven hundred pieces of heavy artillery [are] mounted on the rock. The part of the rock facing the Spanish lines is excavated and guns pointed through port-holes like the side of a ship. You have a fine view of the Spanish coast and mountains from Cape Spartel at the entrance of the gut to Malaga in the Mediterranean and of the Coast of Barbary from Tangier to Tetuan. Opposite Gibraltar is Algeciras in Spain 5 miles distant, the Castle of Almanza, and town of San Roque about the same distance.

An Artificer [was] killed when at work about this time by an ape rolling a stone from the top of the Rock on his head. The Rock abounds with apes of a very large size, some few racoons, foxes and partridges, supposed to come from Spain.

6 August. Had two men killed by falling down the Rock.

10 November. Went to Camp about [? above] the cliffs of the Rock, and all Merchants and other Inhabitants in the Cliffs, to avoid the fire from the Spanish Gunboats and Batteries, as we expected a Siege. A soldier killed in attempting to desert to the enemy.

11 November. Stormy weather; wind west. A Convoy arrived from England with troops; engaged by the Spanish gun-boats, which damaged them much and killed several men on shore.

A Spanish Guard deserted to our Garrison; had to fight their way from the Spanish lines.

12 November. A soldier fell over the line wall and was killed. Two Artificers blown up.

23 December. I was carried to the Navy Hospital in a fever; remained there 14 weeks. Was given up by seven Doctors, but by God's help deceived them all. When lightheaded I frequently saw my Sisters standing by my bedside.

About this time the *Courageux*,* 74, was lost near Gibraltar, and part of her Crew which were saved [were] brought to the hospital where I was, in a very mangled state.

1797.

A fleet of 500 sail of enemy's vessels passed by the Rock. Admiral Sir John Jervis fell in with them and beat them off [Cape] St. Vincent [14 February, 1797.]

1 April. Went to be an Officer's servant for 15 months.

2 April. My birthday.

3 April. A soldier hanged for killing an Italian.

4 April. Went to a Spanish play.

5 April. A soldier shot for desertion.

7 April. Fighting with the Spanish gunboats all day and night to protect a convoy from England.

---

* 10 December, 1796. H.M.S. *Courageux*, 74, temporarily commanded by Lieutenant John Burrows, acting for Captain Benjamin Hallowell, who was on duty ashore, was at anchor in the Bay of Gibraltar. In a gale she " drove from her anchors, brought up almost under the guns of a Spanish Battery on the N.W. side of the Bay, and, when she weighed again and stood towards the African coast, ran on some rocks below Ape's Hill, where in a few minutes, she became a wreck. Of 593 persons who were apparently on board at the time, only 129 escaped." *The Royal Navy. A History.* By W. L. Clowes. Vol. IV. p. 289.

1797.

8 April. Received a letter from my brother for the first time. The enemy killed several men on shore.

16 April. A man of the Artillery drowned.

20 April. A man of the Artillery killed by falling over the Castle ramp. I fell over near the same place myself but a short time before and was much bruised.

21-3 April. Engaged by the Spanish gunboats. They threw a number of shot into the garrison, killed several men, and drove the 42nd Regiment† off the parade where they were at exercise, and knocked down several trees.

27 April. All hands to their alarm post on account of the *Andromache*, Frigate, being engaged in the Bay by 30 Spanish gunboats, at 12 o'clock at night. One of the frigate's guns burst and killed some of her men. General Trigge's* Lady was on board the Frigate, from England.

[These dates, April 21-27, appear to be a month too early. Mr. W. G. Perrin, Librarian at the Admiralty, has kindly looked through the log of H.M.S. *Andromache*, 32, and reports as follows:—On 22 May, 1797, her boats assisted in driving off some Spanish gunboats which were attacking a convoy coming into the Bay of Gibraltar, and on 6 November in that year she took part in what appears to have been a much more serious action in which she was engaged with 14 or 15 of the Spanish gunboats, also while protecting a convoy coming into the Bay. This action seems to have taken place off Algeciras.

The number of boats which attacked on 22 May is not given, but as they seem to have been driven off by three cutters and a gunboat on the English side there cannot, I think, have been very many.]

About this time a great number of duels were fought by Officers of different Regiments. The Captain‡ of the Company [to] which I then belonged fought a duel with a Captain of [the Royal] Engineers and killed him, and was dismissed [from] the service, for it was the 5th Officer he had killed.

1798.

In April, 1798, I entered the Freemasons' Society, and in June was raised to the sublime Degree of Master Mason; in 1799 I was made Royal Arch Super-Excellent Mason. In 1804 I was initiated and dubbed a Knight of that Noble, Holy, Glorious, and Universal Order of Knight Templars, also the Order of Saint John of Jerusalem, Mark Mason and Knight of Malta

[From Records in the Grand Lodge of Freemasons the following information has been furnished:—

"Benjamin Miller, "Soldier," returned as a Member by Lodge No. 220, Provincial Grand Lodge of Gibraltar, in December, 1806. This was under the Antients' (or Athol) Grand Lodge.

---

† The Head Qrs. and 5 Companies had reached Gibraltar in the summer of 1795; the other 5 Companies were stationed in the West Indies.

* Major-General Thomas Trigge was at this time Lieut.-Governor of Gibraltar.

1798.

" Again the same body on 6 November, 1809, granted a warrant to Lodge No. 345 (heretofore No. 5) in the Fourth Battalion, Royal Artillery, at Gibraltar, and, as a Founder and Junior Warden, the name of Benjamin Miller again appears."]

19 October.   Embarked at Gibraltar on board the *Loyal Briton* for the Expedition to take the Island of Minorca.

20 October.   Lord Nelson's Prizes from the Nile* came into the Bay and anchored alongside of us, in a shocking battered state, the British ships equally in as bad state as the prizes, and the blood of the brave men who had fought in them still to be seen on some of the ships

We gave each ship three cheers as they passed us and all the Bands on board the fleet for the Expedition struck up ' Rule Britannia.' The Tars manned their rigging and returned our cheers, and seemed to say, Go, my brave Soldiers, and Imitate your brave Countrymen on the watery Element.

Our anchors were nearly up at the time, so we got under way and soon lost sight of the Rock, and steered our course for Minorca.   A fine breeze; wind north-west.   We passed the Isle of Alboran and the Island of Ivica.

14 Days becalmed off Cape de Gata.§

Captain of the ship killed his Cabin-boy by striking him on the head with a handspike.   [He] was ordered back to England for trial.

4 November.   Sprang up west breeze, and we made way.

5 November.   A Gale.   Our ship sprang her main yard and our long boat broke loose from the deck, and we were all like to be lost by the carelessness of the man at the wheel.

7 November.   Came in sight of the Islands of Minorca and Majorca, and landed immediately under a 4-gun Battery.   But the Spaniards were soon dispersed by the fire of our shipping, very few men lost.

[Captain Framingham was the only officer with the Company. According to the Muster Rolls (P.R.O., W.O. 10/340) for November and December, 1798, the other Officers ' (Captain-Lieutenant Thomas Charleton; 1st Lieutenants William Payne and Thomas S. Hughes) remained at Gibraltar, as well as 88 of other ranks, out of a total strength of 125.]

13 hundred Swiss that were in the Spanish service deserted to us. We lay on the Heights that night and next day [8 November), but got information that the Spanish army were gone, part to Port Mahon† and part to Ciudadela.**

So we marched all this night till we came under Mount Toro (or

---

‡ Captain John Bradbridge, Royal Artillery, was dismissed from the army on 27 September, 1797, for killing Captain-Lieutenant Peter Couture in a duel, on 30 June, 1797. He was succeeded by Captain Haylett Framingham, R.A., who, however, did not join the Company until 4 May, 1798.

* The battle of the Nile was fought on 1 August, 1798.

§ In the province of Almeria (Spain).

† The capital of Minorca, on the E. side of the island.

** On the W. coast of the island.

1798. November.

Mount Bull), near Mercadal.* I got wounded in my left foot this night but would not be persuaded to go back with the rest of the wounded men, but continued the march. Took a great number of prisoners in this town and got plenty of wine, very cheap.

Stayed two days at this place. Then our army was divided, the right wing, to which I belonged, was ordered to Ciudadela and the left wing to Port Mahon, in pursuit of the enemy. We came in view of Ciudadela, [and] lay at a distance for two days, but on the night of 15 November we made large fires to deceive the enemy and stole a silent march within musquet shot of the garrison and began to erect batteries to open on them in the morning. We could have blown the town down in a few hours.

At daylight our General (Stuart) summoned the town to surrender or otherwise he would commence his bombardment, and storm them and put all to the sword. They fired a few shots at us but soon after sent out a flag of truce to surrender, which was a fine thing for the poor inhabitants. We could see them running like mad people, and the tops of the houses and the churches [were] covered with people, as we imagined for the purpose of throwing stones on us if we had stormed the town without firing on it.

So on 17 November, we sent the flank Companies and a part of [our] artillery to take possession of the town and marched the enemy out prisoners of war.

We then drew the remainder of our army back, about half a mile, wh·   ay 3 weeks in ploughed fields, without either house, tent, bush or trees to shelter us from the inclemency of the weather, which was very wet and cold, and a great quantity of thunder and lightning.

I went several times into the town to overhaul the guns and stores.

We found the Minorquins much attached to the English. There was a strong guard of Spaniards left in the town to protect their officers' baggage until it could be put on board. So one day that I was in the town and almost tipsy with drinking wine, a Swiss belonging to the Spanish Guard came to me and made motions that he wanted to desert. Says I ' Corra ' (that is, run). I drew my sword and followed him and put him past the Spanish sentry, who tried to stab him, but I stopped him. At the same time a Spanish officer cut a Drummer to pieces who was trying to desert.

At night, as we were going to our camp, we saw another Swiss soldier crawling on his hands and knees towards our Camp. He had made his escape over the walls, but the rope not being long enough he had strained his legs and could not stand. We carried him to the Camp on our backs. It being a very wet night, and we pretty full of wine, I lay down in the furrow of a ploughed field and slept until morning, when I found myself nearly covered with water and scarcely able to stand, and many more [were] in a worse state than me.

* A village in the centre of the island.

1799.

After breaking up Camp, the Regiment and guns to which I was attached went to a town called Mercadal and Fornella, from whence I was ordered to Allayor, where I remained 9 months.

While I was in this town, one night, when on guard, I dreamed that I was at Yeovil and that my father sent for me. He was dying. I was conducted to a small room at the corner of the market place and found my father on a bed. I thought he rose and took me by the hand and said ' God bless you, Ben, for I must be off,' and he left me. But I followed him. I thought he went into the Church and straight to the altar; he got upon the altar and crept through a hole that was over the altar, and I got on the altar to look after him, but could see him no more. But [I] was quite delighted with the glorious appearance of the place, full of Angels and the most heavenly music I had ever heard. I thought it must be heaven itself.

The clock now struck one and the Serjeant wakened me to go on sentry. I was very melancholy, being wakened from a dream of my dear deceased parent. After I was on sentry I could not refrain from tears.

During our stay at Allayor we were very intimate with the priests and friars who frequently came to our Barracks, and we visited their Convents and Churches, saw them perform High Mass, and administer the Extreme Unction to the sick, when more dead than alive. They are great Bigots. The priest rings a small bell into the ear of the poor deluded person, when struggling for breath, to eat the Holy wafer. I one day asked a Friar of the Franciscan Order what they meant by Confession, doing penance, and giving absolution; or, what right they had to make their flock confess their sins in their ears, make them do penance, and then give them absolution, which they do for a shilling.

He said that every good Christian ought to do it. I asked him if he could show me anything in the Testament to support his pretention. He said he could easily do that, for St. John xx, 23rd verse, says :—" Whosoever sins ye remit, they are remitted unto them; and whosoever sins ye retain, they are retained," and he said I could not contradict it.

I told him that it was not those words, nor any other in St. John, that gave a set of drunken debauched Priests and Friars authority to confess their flock, make them do penance and give them absolution, and if the Testament spoke truth, they would go to hell themselves, if God did not give them remission of sins, although they were priests. I asked where he could find Confession in the ear of Priest or Friar spoken of. He said " St. James, v, verse 16. Confess your faults." I told him that was not St. James's meaning of the words, and if he would look farther he would see the Apostle's meaning. " Confess your faults one to another," which is plain he did not mean Confession to a priest. He said I did not like the doctrine of the Mother Church, so I wanted to fall out with her and him, both, but if I died without confession and absolution I should surely go to Hell.

1799.

I told him I should confess my sins to God, and I hoped he would absolve [me] from all my sins, but before I would give a priest a shilling to confess me I would go and spend it in a halter to hang him.

I asked him where the Testament ordered them to make their flock do penance. He said [that] in the 1st [Epistle to the] Corinthians, 5th chapter, 5th verse, St. Paul says:—

" Deliver such an one to Satan for the destruction of the flesh, that the spirit may be saved in the day of the Lord Jesus."

I told him St. Paul's meaning was not [to] make them do penance. In the 1st Epistle to the Corinthians, 5th chapter, 13th verse, he says:—

" Therefore put away from among yourselves that wicked person." So you are wrong when you take upon your [self to] cause your flock to inflict punishments on their own bodies, for the word is not ' Do penance,' but ' put such a one from among you.' He said penance was a very wholesome discipline and sweared [served] an important end.

Yes, I told him, it did, for it made the people more afraid of the priest than of God himself, for you make them obey you but your penance will not make them obey God, so that penance is more for the benefit of the Clergy than it is to prevent sin. And, where is the need of your absolution? for if God forgives us, what need have we for the absolution of the priest? and, if He does not forgive us, your absolution is of no avail.

He told me I was an obstinate heretic and that England had no need of priests, for their soldiers were all priests and carried the Bible. But, if he had the ruling of people in England he would have all the Bibles burned. But I told him the people in England would burn all the priests first or hang them with their beads. I further told him that their priests and Friars were a set of hypocrites, and their flock a poor weak, blind, deluded set of people to believe in them, and that their Extreme unction, anointing, confession, penance, absolution, and the purgatory, a parcel of absurd* nonsense.

He asked me if I did not believe in purgatory, neither. I told him No, for the Blood of Christ through faith had cleansed us from all sin, which would [not] be the case if any part of it was left for purgatory. This made the old friar shake his head, and said it was of no service to talk to me, [and] that I should next curse the Virgin Mary and all the Saints in Heaven. I told him they were impious in the titles they gave the Virgin Mary, such as Mother of mercy, Refuge of Sinners, Gates of heaven, &c., &c. Our Saviour foresaw the adoration that was likely to be paid to the Virgin and plainly declared against it. See St. Luke's Gospel, xi, 27 verse, and you will there see the same spirit breaking out that now causes so much idolatry among you, and your flock.

" And it came to pass, as he spake these things, a certain woman of the company lifted up her voice and said unto him, Blessed is the womb that bare thee, and the paps which thou hast sucked.

---

* ' Damned ' erased!

1799.

" But he said, Yea rather, blessed are they that hear the word of God, and keep it."

Now by those words Jesus condemned all you that pretend to honour him by worshipping his mother and calling her the Queen of heaven. So your misapplied devotion is condemned by our Lord's own words, and shews you that his mother had no particular privilege above others, but that she heard the word of God and kept it, a blessing which is common to all true believers.

Says I, you give your flock leave to work on the Lord's Day. But they will chop off their arms rather than work on Lady Day, for fear of you making them do penance, which is plain proof that you cause [them] to honour the Clergy more than God himself.

I next asked him what they had done with one of their Commandments which says, " thou shalt not worship any Graven Images," which put Father Antony quite out of countenance. But he said they did not worship them. I told him I saw them no longer ago than yesterday kneeling and praying to wooden Saints, which their churches were full of, and they could find no authority in the word of God for so doing. The friar could find nothing in Scripture to countenance their praying to saints, but the rich man in hell praying to Abraham. I told him the example of a damned Spirit in hell was a bad subject for the pious on earth. He seemed to perceive it in this light, and finding himself quite aground he dropped the subject of religion, and said if the English stayed long in the Island we should set the people against the Clergy and make heretics of them. I told him [that] bad as we were we were much better Christians than they were, and we should strive to enlighten the people as much as possible. I told him their religion was all blindfold absurdity. We had no more at that time.

In January a fever broke out in our army and carried off a great number. A man of the Artillery, being on sentry at a windmill, let it loose, caught hold of one of the vanes, and went round with it but was not hurt.

The part of the army that went to Port Mahon and Fort George took it without opposition.

Four of us went out to an orange grove to steal oranges, but for fear of being caught we split the tree and carried the half of it to the barracks with the oranges growing on it.

About this time, as some soldiers were at work, one of them struck his pickaxe on a bomb shell which lay buried in the ground. The pickaxe struck fire, which communicated to the powder in the shell and burst it, and blew the man to atoms; and a man of the Artillery [was] killed with [? in] a fandango* by the Minorquins.

20 February. A soldier hanged for killing a Minorquin. The commanding officer compelled his brother, who was serjeant in the same Regiment, to go to the awful scene. Our Officer was ordered to return

---

* This is obscure. ' Fandango ' is a popular Spanish dance for two persons. Possibly it means ' whilst dancing a fandango.'

1799.

to Ciudadela. His servant died in the fever, so he took me with him to be his servant. We remained at Ciudadela 4 months. I had the happiest time in this place I ever had in the service; the people were so friendly with us. My master and I lived with a family of Minorquins in this town, who were very fond of me. They had some relations [who were] priests, and one night [when] one of them happened to be there they told him what a number of books my master had and how I was always reading.

They asked me if I would get one and read to them. I had often read Romances to them, which they are very fond of hearing. But I fetched the Bible this time and began reading from it. The Priest said it was not a good book, and after threatening the people he took his hat and went away. They said he was a good man, but I said he was a great rogue and they were fools, which very much offended them.

In March [1799] a man of the Artillery drowned himself. He had took an oath not to drink any wine or other strong liquor for a year, but broke it. He then swore another oath and forfeited it also, which we thought preyed so much on his conscience that made him so rash. He went to the sea side and sat on a high rock and tied a handkerchief so tight round his neck that it may prevent him from swimming, as he was a good swimmer. His Bible was found lying on his jacket at the place [where] we supposed he fell into the water.

I was now ordered to go with my master to Port Mahon and embark on board a Bomb Vessel destined for Malta, but she sailed before our arrival. I rode 36 miles that day on an ass. Mahon is a very fine town, and we found it to be the most fruitful part of the island. Vegetables of all kinds in great plenty, and cauliflowers in abundance, the largest I ever saw. At this place I saw a man that came from Yeovil and several from Ilchester.

After staying at this place about three months we were again ordered back to Ciudadela.

Had a dispute with a friar concerning the forgiveness of murderers if they get to the altar before detected; he said it was sufficient. I told him that if any of them committed murder while the English were there, they would be hanged [even] if they had been at fifty altars. He said that the Bisby* would not allow it. I told him General Stuart† would turn 'Bisby' on such an occasion, which they very soon experienced to their great astonishment, for one of them killed his mother by running a skewer through her tongue and cutting it out by the root. They were trying him by the 'Bisby' and Clergy, and cleared him to do penance, but General Stuart, being aware of their mode of proceeding, collected the number of Officers that usually sit on such occasions. They went to the Convent and waited quietly until he was ordered to do penance, when he ordered the 'Bisby' from his seat, although a Roman Catholic himself, placed his officers and sat as judge himself, and condemned the prisoner to be hanged by the neck until dead, and afterwards, his body

* This must be the soldier's vernacular for the Spanish *Bispo*—a Bishop.
† The *Hon.* Sir Charles Stuart. See 'D.N.B.'

1799.

to be given to a Surgeon for dissection. A few days after he was brought to the gallows, attended by a priest, who told him that he had nothing to fear for the rope would break if he was an hundred times hanged, as he was only condemned by heretic laws (as we were told afterwards). But the priest seemed rather doubtful as to the virtue of the cord, I thought, for he gave the malefactor the Sacrament and absolution under the gallows, after which he was turned off, and another man ordered to get on his shoulders, which made the priest look very foolish in the eyes of the bigoted multitude.

When the priest wants to deceive the people by telling them the halter will break, they use *aqua fortis* on some part of the rope, so that it breaks when strained, but the English provost-marshal brought a halter with him and entirely confuted his plan.

In September, 1799, I and 15 more gunners volunteered for the Expedition to Egypt and marched all night for Port Mahon. Not one of the 15 escaped either being killed or wounded.

On our arrival at Mahon we were ordered on board the *Monarch**
to join a detachment of the Company we belonged to. Being very dirty with the march, [we] jumped overboard to wash ourselves. While bathing we were called on board and ordered to pack our knapsacks and go on board the *Indefatigable*. We set sail and steered our course for Gibraltar.

While lying in Gibraltar Bay, one man died. He was brought on the forecastle and laid on a grating. I won 8 dollars at cards that day, and the man that I won it from would not let me be quiet, but we must go and play by moonlight, and I chanced to sit on the dead man not knowing he was there until one of my comrades asked me if I was not ashamed of myself to sit on the dead man to play cards. I found my mistake and shifted. The man could only get back one dollar of his money, and I made a promise never more to play for money, which I have fulfilled.

[The year 1800 commences somewhere about here.]

1800.

From Gibraltar we sailed for Tetuan in Africa to take in water. From Tetuan back to Gibraltar, where we were joined by a large fleet from England, loaded with troops.

Sailed again for Tetuan. Was drove from our anchors in a gale of wind. Strove to put into Gibraltar Bay, but the fog was so thick, and night coming on, we could not see the land on either side. Lost several ships that ran against the Rock.

So we bore away through the Gut at the rate of 14 knots an hour, under storm stay-sails. When we came to Cape Spartel our ship hove to and was near lost, through a large Troop-ship which had a whole Regiment on board. I was between decks at the time. It was shocking to hear the cries of the women and the men all in confusion. Two men that were lying in the berth with me ran upon deck to jump over-board, but I lay still, and listened to hear the awful crash when the two ships

1800.

would come in contact with each other. But through the activity of our boatswain in jumping to the helm, and putting our ship about, we only lost some of our after-rigging and stern-works by the broadside of the other ship running across us, and to my great joy I heard our Captain say ' Thank God all is safe.' If it had not been God's pleasure that one of the artillery should see something like a cloud through the darkness of the night approaching our ship, who told the boatswain, both ships must have gone to the bottom and about 1,200 people drowned, for the sea ran mountains high, and [it was] as dark as pitch.

Our Captain saw the Commodore's light at a great distance, and our ship being the best sailor in the fleet, he was determined to follow him and get out of the fleet to prevent further danger. So we kept close to the Commodore drifting under storm stay-sails for 14 days on the Atlantic Sea. But the gale abating we bore for the Gut of Gibraltar, and found great part of the fleet at anchor near Sallee, on the North-west coast of Barbary.

Next morning, wind west—a gentle gale. We got under way and went back to Tetuan, on the north coast of Barbary. Completed watering and sailed for Gibraltar. Collected the fleet and sailed through the Gut towards Cadiz. [2 October, 1800.] Anchored off Cadiz and made ready for landing. We were in the boats and rowing towards land two days running, under fire of a Battery. But the Spaniards sent out a boat with a flag of truce and ransomed the town.† We then returned to Gibraltar, where we received orders to sail for Egypt. I was ordered to go on board the *Thames*, transport, with the remainder of my detachment. Here we threw one of our men overboard.

1 November. Sailed for Tetuan.

5. Weighed anchor and sailed up the Mediterranean.

7. Passed the island of Ivica. A conductor of stores thrown overboard.

10. Passed between the Islands of Minorca and Majorca and entered the Gulf of Lyons; very rough sea. A boy was washed from the deck, and left again on deck by the same wave.

11. Two cocks were fighting on deck; one jumped overboard.

13. A goat jumped overboard and was drowned. Dead calm for 4 days.

18. The same ship that was so near running us down, ran foul of a brig and sunk her. Eight Artillerymen, a boy, a woman, and child were drowned.

19. Came in sight of the islands of Corsica, Elba, and Sardinia. Lost the fleet. Came in sight of Malta Light-house in the night, and lay to; very high sea.

20. At day light a frigate came and towed us into Malta harbour.

21. I was ordered to join the boat's crew with 5 more who could

† The Fleet was under the command of Admiral Lord Keith. Clowes's *History of The Royal Navy.* IV. 425.

1800.

row in the boat, for the purpose of putting the officers on shore when wanted.

23 November. I and another man took an Officer on shore. Very wet day, which caused us to go to a wine-house, where we got drunk. It rained four hours with such rapidity that it washed the cats and dogs from the street into the sea. I was nearly washed away in saving a cat when drunk. On our coming to the boat it was sunk with the quantity of rain that fell. It took us till near night to clear the boat, after which we put to sea, but being both so very drunk we could not find our ship. A serjeant and party of men were sent in a boat in search of us, and took us on board prisoners, but when we got on board the Officers took compassion on us being so wet and cold, [that] they sent me to bed and gave me a bottle of rum, but put the other man in irons for being saucy. I was not to go in the boat any more.

26. We were all ordered to land at Fort Angelo.* We were greatly surprised to find everything so cheap, especially bread and wine, for wine was not one penny per quart, which appeared to us very strange, as the French army had so lately left it.

28. I, and two more got leave to go over to the City of Valetta, the most beautiful place I ever saw. We went to St. John's Church and saw where the great Bonaparte stole the Gold gates from before the altar: the beauty and splendour of it is past my ability to express. We also saw the Armoury, and Council Chamber, or Grand Lodge room, of the Holy order. The time stole so insensibly away that we did not get to the wharf till it was quite dark, and the sea was so rough that we could not get a boat man to take us across, but we jumped into a boat, me and another, and put to sea. We had not got twenty yards before the boat upset and both of us would have been drowned if we had not been good swimmers.

When we came near the wharf there was a number of Officers waiting for boats, but could get none that would go. They cried out, pull out them men, they will be drowned. I lost my hat and feather in the water, and when I got on shore I began to pull off my sword and coat to jump in again to try if I could find it. An Officer laid hold of me and said I should not go. Did I want to be drowned? But I got from him and jumped in, but could not find my hat. So we got a boat at last to take us across. Next day [29 November] I had the ague very bad.

30 November. We were ordered to embark, and it happened well that I was sick or I should have been in an hobble for losing my hat and feather. But one of our men died soon after, so I got his hat and the Serjeant told the Officers that mine was blown overboard.

A few days after we embarked I was again ordered to join the Boat's Crew, which I was very happy for, as I had an opportunity of going ashore at every place we put in at, but took care not to get drunk any more.

We saw Mount Eatney [Etna], one of the burning mountains in the

---

* On the East side of the Grand Harbour.

1800.

Isle of Sicily, which is but a short distance from Malta. I also saw the place where St. Paul had the fire when he shook the viper from his hand; the spot is held in great veneration by the Maltese.

[From this point onwards to the re-embarkation of the Expeditionary Army—1 October, 1801—at the conclusion of the Egyptian campaign, the dates and occurrences as given by Miller, have been checked with the *Journal of the late Campaign in Egypt*, etc., by Captain Thomas Walsh, 93rd Foot, published in 1803—pp. 42 to 223—on which latter the author writes that " the long hovering dove at length found a place for the sole of her foot." There are very few points of difference.]

On 20 December, 1800, the signal was made for to get under way at night; 3 men fell over-board fighting, but [were] not drowned.

1801.

January. Came in sight of the Island of Crete and Rhodes; dreadful rough weather; passed through the Gulf of Venice and saw where the brass Colausious [? Colossus] stood.

February. Entered Marmorice Bay,† in Asia. This place is inhabited by Turks, and the same place where the French fleet hid from Lord Nelson's fleet. Here we put all our sick on shore in camp. The remainder of the army were employed in getting wood, water, taking Turkish horses on board, and going on shore for exercise. This country abounds with wild beasts; it was very dismal to hear them at night from the shipping. A wolf of an enormous size used to come and howl from a rock down over the tents where the sick men lay; they were obliged to keep large fires all night to keep off the beasts. Two men and one woman were devoured by the wild beasts through straggling too far into the woods. Their clothes and part of their bones were afterwards found.

In February a hail storm.* Some of the hail stones were taken up which measured an inch square: [they] broke the skylight on the Quarter-decks of the ships.

25 February. [22 February according to Walsh.] Weighed anchor and put to sea.

27. Passed the Isle of Cyprus, and put across for Egypt; a very rough passage. We lost nearly all our small vessels and Gunboats in the passage, but they most of them joined afterwards in Aboukir Bay.

1 March. Came in sight of Alexandria and anchored in Aboukir Bay.

4 March. Signal for landing, but came on a heavy gale and rough sea. Some of the fleet were forced to put to sea. The ship that I was in struck three times on the same sandbank which the *Culloden*, one of Nelson's ships, struck on at the time of action just opposite Aboukir Castle. [1 August, 1798.]

On 7 March, at night, the signal was made to land next morning and all the light vessels to get as near shore as possible.

---

† Marmorice, on the coast of Anatolia, in Asia Minor, about 40 miles N. of Rhodes. Lat. 36° 32′ N., Long. 28° 31′ E. The Fleet reached Marmorice on 29 December, 1800, and 1 January, 1801. Miller appears to be a month late in his dates.

* Walsh records this as occurring on 9 February.

1801.

At 2 o'clock in the morning [8 March] we were all in the boats with 3 days' provisions in our haversacks, but many brave fellows never had the pleasure of using it. We made towards the land, which we reached at daylight, within about a mile. Formed the boats in line and began to cheer; 14 pieces of small French cannon playing on us for three quarters of an hour, before we could get on shore, cut our boats in pieces and a number of men. At last we landed on the point of the French soldiers' bayonets, for they came close to the water's edge and killed some of our men coming out of the boats, but they saw we were determined, and sought their safety in flight. We gave three cheers and followed them until the evening. A great number of men [were] lost on both sides.

On the beach where we landed we piled up no less than 200 human skulls in the space of a few hundred yards, supposed to be the bones of the men who fell in Nelson's engagement.

We lay quiet until the 13th, when the French again gave us battle, but we drove them close under the walls of Alexandria. We lost a deal of men on both sides. It was a running fight from daylight until dusk in the evening.

After the battle was over we retreated about a mile to take possession of an height. We had no water. I went out with a watering party but was drove back by the French picquets.

On 18 March the 12th and 26th Light Dragoons went out to meet a party of French, but got cut to pieces. Nothing but skirmishing with the out-posts till the 21st, when the French army 14,000 strong came out on us about an hour before day-light with great fury, making sure to beat us back and drown us in the lake. They made three desperate charges on us, but were repulsed as often. One man of the 42nd Regiment ran his bayonet through five Frenchmen one after the other (as they were entering some old ruins at Nicopolis Heights) but was killed immediately after.

They charged one of our batteries after our ammunition was done and would have killed every man. They gave some of the gunners shocking cuts. I was cut in both legs. But the gallant 42nd came to our assistance and killed every Frenchman that was in the Battery. So Bony's invincible army were obliged to show us their backs, leaving between 4 and 5,000 dead on the field, and had we not run short of ammunition they must all have been cut off.

We lost a great number, no less than 60 Artillery men killed and wounded, but our loss was nothing to the loss of the enemy. Sir Ralph Abercromby fell in this battle.

A parley for two days to bury the dead. We put 200 Frenchmen, besides Englishmen and horses, in one hole, where they lay thickest.

A few days after the battle I took a solitary walk amongst the scattered graves to ruminate on the implacable lot of men until I would come to some of my companion's graves. And, thinks I, here lie the

mangled remains of a comrade, who but the other day, he and I were
very jovial, drinking wine together, and perhaps the next destructive day
of carnage it may be my lot at no great distance from this awful spot to
be laid where no relation or friend will ever have the melancholy
satisfaction to drop the sympathetic tear. Then I would reflect how
dreadful it was to be cut off so suddenly, and so neglectful as soldiers
are in regard of religion. But, a soldier's life of honour is subject to so
many changes that he has not time to think of religion like another man,
for no sooner, perhaps, does he think of prayer than the drum beats or
trumpets sound to arms—and how can he talk of forgiving his enemy
when it is his whole duty to destroy them.

SKETCH MAP OF LOWER EGYPT TO SHOW RELATIVE POSITIONS OF
PLACES NAMED IN THE TEXT.

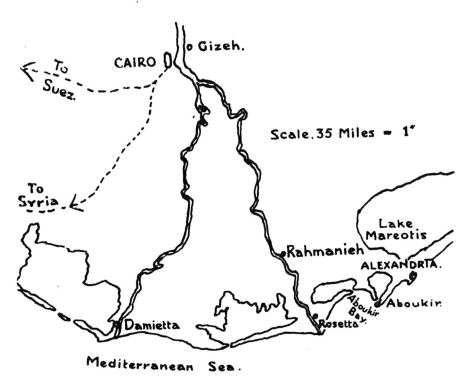

After this battle our camp was dressed up in awful grandeur, for we
brought all the Frenchmen's hats, caps, and helmets, and stuck them on
pikes and poles in front of the tents, some covered with blood and some
full of hair, skull, and brains of the late unfortunate wearer. We now
began to cut sluices and let the sea in to all the low parts of the country

1801. April.

to prevent the French from leaving Alexandria, or receiving reinforcements from Grand Cairo, by which means we soon saw a fleet of armed vessels on the plains, where but a short time before we had fought a general engagement.

29 April. A very heavy rain, the only rain while in the country.

Beginning of May. The hot winds began. We could scarcely bear our heads out of the tents. The Arabs frequently drop dead in the market place with it. Our army began to take the plague of the eyes. I was obliged to go 16 days to the hospital tent with it. We also began to be very lousy.

4 June. I marched with part of the Army for Grand Cairo, about 150 miles up the country. I was in a very bad state of health, but would not stay behind. We left Troops sufficient at Alexandria to keep the enemy at bay that was in that City.

On our first day's march, a fox ran through our army, which made the soldiers say we were to have a fox chase as well as a French chase, but if they ran as fast as it did we should never catch them.

On the 5th we passed two villages, surrounded with mud walls. As we came nigh them we heard a great noise, much like the noise of turkey cocks, but as we came nearer we perceived it to be some hundreds of women's heads looking over the walls, warbling [? wobbling.] their tongues in a very ridiculous manner—their fashion of saluting of us, so we displayed our Colours, and the Bands [were] ordered to play.

6 June. Passed Rosetta, and pitched our Camp at Rahmanieh, a strong inland fort on the left bank of the Nile. We found a strong party of the enemy here who gave us battle. Killed a Colonel of Artillery, and a number of our men. But they made large fires in the night to deceive us and went off for Cairo. We got a store of French clothing at this place which cost several men their lives, for the Turks saw some of them straggling and took them for French soldiers, having part of their clothing on, and cut their heads off. It was horrid to see the savage Turks come into the camp with the poor Frenchmen's heads tied together by the hair and thrown across the saddle, and one or two in each hand streaming with blood. They had five dollars from the Basha for each head.

One day after an engagement, we saw a Turk going to kill some poor wounded Frenchmen, but our General ordered one of our Dragoons to go and cut him down, which he did.

8. We went in pursuit of the enemy past several miserable towns and villages. We frequently thought that we were coming to a large body of water or sea, until our guides told us it was only the appearance [of] the country by the sun reflecting on the sand, which always deceives travellers not accustomed to the Country.

9. When halted for the day and just beginning to cook our meat (buffalo flesh) the trumpet sounded to strike our tents for a forced march. Enemy in sight, and we soon fell in with, and took a party of French and 500 camels loaded with provisions for Alexandria.

1801.

10 June. Halted at Damietta.

[This is an obvious mistake. On 9 and 10 June, the army halted at Burlos, a village on the L. bank of the Nile, about 10 miles from Grand Cairo.]

11. Came again on the banks of the Nile and bathed in it for the first time.

12. Passed an English soldier with his head cut off. Went to a village to buy milk. The women all ran away as soon as they saw us, which did not grieve us much for they are quite frightful. Some of them are entirely naked, except their face, which they cover with a piece of cloth, and holes cut in it for the mouth, nose and eyes, but before we left the country some of them were not afraid to show their pretty faces. They are marked on the chin, cheeks, nose, forehead, and arms with Indian ink, and look more like blue-faced monkeys than human beings.

[Walsh described the Mahomedan women whom he saw at Marmorice in much the same uncomplimentary terms:—

" Few women are ever to be seen, and even then are so muffled up and concealed in long vestments as to leave nothing perceptible but their eyes, which are so ugly as to suppress any desire of seeing the rest of their persons."]
Came in sight of the pyramids.

13. Came in sight of more pyramids. This day I took very ill and a Dragoon's horse was sent back for me to ride, which I could scarcely do. There was also a Non-Commissioned officer and two men to guard me and get me along, as it was dangerous of being killed by the Arabs if we stopped in the rear, which I should not have cared much for [i.e. much minded] at that time I was in such pain.

14. I was much better and marched again. Passed a number of towns and the people brought boiled eggs, melons, and cakes fried with oil for sale.

15. Came to camp in front of Grand Cairo where we found the French safe in Garrison. Three men drowned in the river Nile striving to save each other.

17. Went to see the Pyramids, and went to the top of the largest; it is supposed to be a mile round it and room at the top to turn a coach and four. One man fired a pistol from the top, but the ball struck on the side before it came to the bottom. I likewise went and saw Joseph's well.

The Turkish army came in front of Gizeh also, but on the other side of the Nile 100,000 strong, and a great number of Mamelukes mounted on dromedaries, fine looking fellows.

18. Five Turks' heads cut off and put between their legs, for forcing an English sentry, that was placed on a bridge of boats, to prevent any of them from coming to our side. Two soldiers of the Queen's Regiment had their heads cut off by the Arabs when out viewing the Pyramids. A man of the Artillery had a narrow escape. A party of Turks were in the act of cutting his head off when dressing himself after

1801. June.

bathing in the Nile, but was rescued by some sailors who fortunately were coming up the river in a boat. Our General made complaint to the Basha, and told him if he did not cause the Turks to desist from their barbarous treatment to the British soldiers, that all the influence he had with them would not prevent the whole British army from turning against the Turks and destroy[ing] them all. The Basha then gave orders for the Turks to bring their prisoners alive and they should have 6 dollars instead of 5.

About this time [23 June] the French capitulated and we took possession of Grand Cairo. There was a gun at this place which [was] fired every day by the reflection of the sun through a glass.

Grand Cairo, Gizeh, and vicinity is 10 miles in length, the capital of Egypt. Another soldier drowned. I went to several large towns, and to several of their coffee houses [to] buy some coffee. The Turks frequent these houses in the same manner as we do our inns but instead of liquors, wine or beer, they sit on mats in groups and drink coffee, and smoke themselves drunk by mixing opium with their tobacco, and you will frequently see a dozen of them lying quite senseless on the floor.

I was now ordered to join the horse artillery guns to act with the Dragoons.

[These were not really " Horse Artillery " guns, but merely guns drawn by horses in improvised fashion in the field.

The following extract from a *Memorandum of Artillery arrangements, etc., on the Expedition to Egypt*, 1801, by Brig.-General Robert Lawson, who was in command of the Artillery, explains the situation : —

" Our Cavalry, from their want of proper horses, being found very unequal to the capitally mounted French Dragoons, it became necessary to aid that defect by the attachment of Artillery. Four light 3-prs. (brought from Malta) were first prepared for this service; their original mode of travelling with shafts and single line of draught was altered to a double one by cutting off the shafts of the limber at the cross-bar, and introducing a pole instead of them, together with other improvements. Four or six horses, with two drivers (according to the ground) drew the carriage. These pieces were served by four Artillerymen—two on the carriage, and two mounted on the off-draught horses. They went through the service to Grand Cairo, and travelled much better than was expected from the lowness of the limber wheels, which defect there was no remedy for in Egypt.

" Four light 6-prs. upon block-trailed carriages, with two royal howitzers, were also equipped (as nearly as the means would admit) for Horse Artillery service. Seven Artillerymen and three drivers, with ten horses, were allotted for the service of each piece—the gunners riding the horses in draught, but the non-commissioned officer mounted single, for the purpose of advancing to examine roads, reconnoitring the enemy, &c."

See *Proceedings of the Royal Artillery Institution*, 1884. XII. pp. 207-20.]

1801. July.

All mounted [men] were employed in taking some Turkish guns down to the Depot on the banks of the Nile, to show them our method of embarking, and conveying guns. The Turkish Colonel of artillery (who was a German and could speak English), gave us a Turkish repast, which consisted of boiled rice and slices of frizzled mutton. The rice was turned out into a large brass vessel as big as a vat for cooling beer; the fat was thrown over it and the slices of mutton placed round the edges of the vessel. We all sat down on the ground round it in the tent, about 20 in number, Turks and English. We had neither knife, fork, or spoon. After we had done, the Turkish Colonel said "You English would like some wine, or beer, but there is our beer," pointing to the river Nile. On our return to camp, about midnight, I had occasion to stop behind the party, when I was attacked by about a hundred wild wolf-dogs. They bit my horse's heels and beset him in such manner that he could not stir, so I was obliged to dismount and draw my sword, holding my horse by the reins, but they were so frightened at the sword that I could only kill one of them, and they all left me. I was greatly afraid I must have left my horse to clear myself. The Serjeant missing me, sent a man back in search of me. I had not gone far before I heard him calling for me and met him immediately. I told him I had lost my sword-scabbard, in a fray with the dogs. He said he would ride to the place with me and try to find it. We went to the place as near as I could judge, being very dark, and dismounted. Soon found it and mounted our horses, when we were both attacked by the dogs, and they would have devoured both horses if we had not dismounted and beat them off with our swords. We did not get up with the party until we got to camp, about 10 miles.

The Nile now began to overflow so that we were ordered to march the French prisoners down the country to Rosetta in order to be sent to France.

A large army joined us at Cairo from Bombay, and Madras, chiefly sepoys.

[This force under the command of Major-General David Baird, arrived on 7 August, and encamped on the island of Roda, on the Nile, near Cairo. It consisted of about 1,000 European and 2,000 Native Troops. The force, however, was too late to take part in the campaign.]

On the march we were obliged to go between the French army and the Turks, or else they would have destroyed the poor Frenchmen. The Turks said, "Francies and Englie, sowie, sowie," that is both alike, because we did not cut their heads off when we took them prisoners, but we aggravated them by telling them the Turk, camel, and buffalo were "sowie, sowie."

As we halted to let the French prisoners pass, for our army to get between them and the Turks, we expected they would give us battle, for they were 6 hours in marching past us, but if they had been so foolish they would all have been killed, for our army was drawn up in order of battle, guns loaded and matches lighted.

1801. August.

On this march we suffered for want of water, for the Nile water was very muddy by the flood coming on. I began to be very tired of horse soldiering for after we halted we had often 10 or 12 miles to go for forage, then feed our horses, and perhaps 2 or 3 miles to go to the Nile to water them before we could look to ourselves, which would be frequently very late at night, and next morning up by two o'clock, and formed into line 2 hours before other soldiers were out of [their] tents.

I was, at this time, wearing a canvas frock for a shirt, all my shirts being either lost or worn out, and when I had time would go and wash it, and stockings in the Nile, and bathe myself while it would dry.

On our arrival at Rosetta all the worst of our horses were shot, and replaced with the horses taken from the French, chiefly Arabians. I had a fine Arabian grey delivered to me, but a party of Artillery being wanted to go to join at Alexandria to besiege it, I volunteered to go with them. On our march to Alexandria we had to behold a dismal sight, for the beach was covered with imputrid dead bodies, some that had been conveyed on board after the battles who had been thrown over board, after dying in their wounds, some that had been thrown into the Nile at Cairo, and on the march which died in the plague that raged in the Turkish army, were brought down by the flood, and great numbers that had been drowned crossing the bar from the mouth of the Nile to Aboukir bay. The smell, and the quantity of flies made the march very disagreeable. The flies were so numerous that at times they quite darkened the air and appeared like a black cloud before us.

While at Grand Cairo we went to the harvest field. Their grain is very fine, but they are very careless and slovenly with it, for they pack it up loose on camels' backs, and the half of it is shook out by the way. They carry it in that manner to a place near a village and throw it in a heap as high as a hay stack, and instead of thrashing it in a barn, they drive cattle and asses round it until it is entirely trodden under foot, which is their manner of thrashing, so that more than half the grain is lost in going between the field, and the thrashing floor. We were nearly over shoe in fine wheat.

One day as one of our camel drivers was loading his camel, the animal took the driver's head in his mouth and bit it in two and killed him dead on the spot.

On our arrival at the army before Alexandria we received orders to embark for the west side of Alexandria. We were at work night and day getting guns, stores, and ammunition on board, and embarked the 3rd day our selves* and sailed up the Lake† in the night. This was a plain on 13 March on which we fought and gained a victory. As we passed the French lines in the night they fired a few shot at us, at which time our army in front of Alexandria, engaged them to draw their attention from us.

The next morning we got [to] the back side of the city, about 7 miles distant, and began to land. A large column of the enemy and some field-pieces came down to the water's edge to oppose our landing,

---

* Embarked 16 August, 1801. *Walsh*, p. 200.   † Mareotis.

1801. August.

but soon retired without firing a shot. Here we were joined by six Regiments and two Companies of Artillery from England.

In the evening we advanced towards the French lines, when Sir Sidney Smith,† his orderly Dragoon, a General, and his Aide-de-Camp, were like to have been shot by some French sharp shooters, who were hid behind a sand bank. Soon after we advanced, I was ordered to join a party that was going to bombard the island and castle of Marabout.* This island is about musquet shot from the land, fortified with a strong castle and batteries, besides 4 large vessels each carrying six guns, which were between us and the island. We worked hard all night in getting our guns down and building a sand-bag battery. By daylight we had all ready, and opened on them with 12 guns and mortars, for about an hour. The enemy returned our fire very smartly, and made the grape and case shot fly among us, and rattle against our guns and wheels like showers of hailstones. I got a thump in my nose with a small stone which was struck by a shot, but we soon sunk three of their gun-vessels and disabled the other, and dismounted most of their guns on the battery. We then began to bombard the Castle. I went outside of our battery to wash my face (which was covered with blood) in the sea, when a whole charge of grape shot came among my feet, and spattered the salt water all over me. We at last had the pleasure to see the castle fall to the ground, and we heard our army give three cheers. We began to prepare to join the army, and marched at 2 o'clock in the morning. But I having a swelling (a common disorder in Egypt) under my left arm, and [feeling] sleepy and tired, having been two nights and two days hard at work on the battery, without sleep or food, was not able to keep up with the party, but lost myself in the deserts and was going to lay down under a sand-hill until daylight, but hearing some beast make a noise like the yawn of a wolf, close by me, I was terrified and thought I should be immediately devoured; the cold sweat ran off me by streams. But finding it had not smelled me I began to move off all of a tremble. I wandered about for some time not knowing where I was going. At last I came to the foot of a *mountain* that ran along the lake side. I got on the top of it and thought I would sit down till daylight. I pulled off my shoes and shook the sand from them. I then got up and took another ramble, until I thought I saw a man, which I suspected to be a sentry from the enemy's picquet, but he challenged me in English. I went up to him and found it to be one of my own party. He told me they had all lost themselves, and were laid down to sleep till it was light; he said there was another man missing besides me. It was now getting light. I sat down about half an hour, and we then proceeded to the camp. On our approach near the tents of the out-piquets, we were surprised at seeing the tracks of wild beasts as thick as the tracks of sheep near a pen fold. The Picquet told us they had been obliged to keep a fire all night, to keep

† Captain Sir William Sidney Smith, Royal Navy, who was in command of a body of 1,000 seamen, serving on land.
* On the shore of the Mediterranean Sea, 7 miles due W. from Alexandria.

them off. It was thought that the smell of of us and our provisions had
brought them from the deserts, as they were never known to come in
such numbers in that quarter before.

On our arrival at camp we found the other man that was lost; he
had found his way in the night by a difficult track.   We joined our
respective guns, and on 22 August we again attacked the enemy, and
drove them into Alexandria, on the western side; our troops on the east
side attacked and beat them in to the East Gate, so that they could get
no succour from any quarter. We now began to erect Mortar Batteries
to bombard Alexandria. They sallied out on us one night, but were
soon driven back.   One poor old grey-headed Frenchman, not being
able to keep up with the rest, fell on his knees and begged for mercy,
but an English soldier, more like a savage than a man, ran him through
with his bayonet. Our soldiers all cried " shame " at him.

I and 4 more gunners were ordered to go and take charge of some
Redoubt batteries called Cleopatra's Batteries near Pompey's Pillar,
which we had taken from the French. Pompey's Pillar is called one of
the wonders of the world, as well as the Pyramids.

[Pompey's Pillar is described by Walsh in these words : —
" This most magnificent Column is situated on a height about $\frac{1}{4}$ of
a mile South of the Old Walls of Alexandria. It is of very beautiful
red Granite and composed of only three pieces, viz., the Capital, Shaft,
and Pedestal. It belongs to the Corinthian order. It is very well pre-
served except on the South and on the North East side. Some signs
of a Greek inscription are still perfectly discernable on the West side,
altho' so much damaged as not to be able to decypher it.   We have
nothing but the most feeble conjecture concerning the construction of this
superb monument; some authors having ascribed it to Cæsar, and others
to Alexander Severus, or to Adrian : it is therefore dangerous to hazard
an opinion upon the subject. The Pedestal is considered to be deficient
in height and the column leans a little to the South West. The following
are the dimensions of this pillar as taken by several of the French Savans,
who accompanied Buonaparte to Egypt, and though they differ materially
from Norden or Pocock's accounts, yet as these authors only measured
it in a hurry and from the shadow, it is but reasonable to give the
preference to persons who, being in possession of the country and having
all the necessary means and implements, must be allowed to be the best
able to give them. I have therefore put it down according to them, in
French measure. The Pedestal is 10 feet, the base 5 feet 6 inches; the
shaft 63 feet 1 inch; the Capital 9 feet 10 inches, and the diameter of the
Column 8 feet 4 inches at the bottom. The Cap of Liberty was placed
on the capital by the Savans when they measured it, having got to the
summit by means of a kite."

The illustration was drawn by Walsh himself and shows the Cap of
Liberty as mentioned by Miller.

Another reference to the Cap of Liberty is found in a *History of*

POMPEY'S PILLAR.

1801. September.

the British Expedition to Egypt, by R. T. Wilson. 1803. 2nd edition.
p. 221 : —

" From several grooves and pieces of iron found by a party of
English sailors, who, in order to drink a bowl of punch, ascended to the
top, by flying a kite and fastening a rope round the capital, scarcely a
doubt can remain of a statue having been formerly erected there . . . . .
A cap of Liberty was substituted by the French, which probably is by
this time taken down."

A foot-note to this paragraph says that " An English Officer of
Marines afterwards ascended and took the cap down."]

At these batteries we found horse-flesh hung up like joints of beef,
and some of it over the fire in pots and pans, boiling and frying.

We had now quite subdued the whole French army, and marched
them on board, prisoners of war. So much for Bony's Invincible army,
which entered Egypt upwards of 40,000 strong. I remained at Pompey's
Pillar 21 days, and had the comfort of pulling off my clothes at night,
the first time for seven months, except when I went to bathe, for it was
against orders to strip at night. The Officers made a paper kite for the
purpose of taking the French cap of Liberty from Pompey's Pillar. They
flew the paper kite over the pillar with a ball of twine fastened to the tail,
and when the twine came immediately over the column they fastened a
large rope to it, and drew it over the top of the column and fastened it
round the bottom of the pillar on one side, so that a man could climb
up by the other.

A large magazine blew up at Fort Triangle near Alexandria, and
killed 15 Artillerymen. A great number of our army died in the plague
about this time; it came with a swelling in the throat, groin, and under
the arms.

On 30 September we received orders to march to the Depot, and on
1 October, 1801, the greatest part of the army embarked, some lamenting
the loss of their wives, women their husbands, and children their fathers
and mothers, and the whole of their companions which were lost, some
in battle, and some by the plague, which greatly damped their joy, and
withered the hard-fought-for laurels, gained on this memorable expedition. A number of watery and melancholy looks towards the shore were
to be seen, as we rowed towards the shipping.

In the evening we set sail, and in 21 days† came in sight of Malta,
throwing dead men overboard almost every day. A few leagues from
Malta we met a French ship of war bearing French, English, and Spanish
colours. Our Commodore hailed them; the Captain said he was going
to Alexandria with news of peace* with all nations. Our Commodore
told him it had been queer peace with us lately, and he must therefore
go back to Malta with him, but on entering Malta harbour we found it
was peace, which greatly surprised us. The French ship was then permitted to go to Egypt.

---

† *i.e.* about 21 or 22 October, 1801.
* The so-called Peace of Amiens, which was ratified on 25 March, 1802.

1801. November.

After we had rode quarantine, we landed a few days to have the shipping cleaned and fumigated. I then embarked on board the *Minotaur*, 74, for Minorca, where we arrived in November, 1801. [Anchored in Port Mahon harbour on 11 November.] I was then Officer's Mess waiter.

I went eight miles to see John Cheffey, a native of Yeovil, the man who enlisted me, but when I came to the place instead of finding John. I met his brother Amos, who told me John was killed in Egypt. Three men drowned in getting plunder from a wreck and several more narrowly escaped the same fate.

1802.

We remained in Minorca 7 months and then gave the island up to the Spaniards, at which the inhabitants were much grieved.

[See *The Lost Possessions of England.* By W. F. Lord. 2nd edition. 1898. Chapter IV. pp. 98-158. The chapter concludes thus:—

" On June 16, 1802, under the provisions of the Peace of Amiens, we handed over Minorca to Spain, and finally evacuated the fortress we had so long held and thrice defended."

The record of places in the Mediterranean garrisoned by England in the course of the last two hundred years, therefore, runs as follows:—

1661-84.	Tangier.	1798-1800.		Gibraltar and Minorca.
		1800-2.	,,	Minorca and Malta.
1684-1704.	No base.			
1704-13.	Gibraltar.	1802-11.	,,	and Malta.
		1811-4.	,,	Malta and Sicily.
1713-56.	,, and Minorca.			
1756-63.	,,	1815-63.	,,	Malta and The Ionian Isles.
1763-82.	,, and Minorca.	1863-79.	,,	and Malta.
		1879-82.	,,	Malta and Cyprus.
1782-94.	,,			
1794-7.	,, and Corsica.	1882-95	,,	Malta, Cyprus and Alexandria.]

We embarked on board the *Monarch*,‡ with orders to sail for England. We then thought our hardships all over but were greatly deceived, for having occasion to put in at Gibraltar, the Duke of Kent* ordered two Companies of Artillery to land, which we thought the unhappiest day we ever saw, for we did not like the place.

We landed on 5 July, 1802,§ and remained there 6 years, after being made believe we were going to England.

‡ The *Monarch* was a Board of Ordnance Transport.
§ This date is confirmed by the Muster Roll of the Company for July, 1802 (P.R.O.— W.O. 10/454).
* H.R.H. Edward, Duke of Kent, who had recently been appointed Governor of Gibraltar. (24 March, 1802.)

1802.   July.

We found the Duke to be very sharp and duty very hard in this Garrison. Frequently saw five men tied up and flogged all together by the tap of the drum, for very small crimes.

In September, 1802, a Serjeant whose wife had lately died, went to the Burying ground, sat down on her grave, and blew out his brains with a pistol. About this time a number of soldiers made away with themselves by shooting, hanging, and cutting their throats, and many deserted to the Spaniards. Two men blown from a gun at a field-day—one of them killed and the other [had] both arms blown off. I got my foot crushed to pieces and was carried to the hospital. A Portuguese frigate wrecked at the back of the rock and many of the crew lost—a dismal sight.

The troops being tired of the severity of the Duke of Kent, the Scotch Royal,† the Regiment he commanded, broke out in open rebellion against him, on 24 December, 1802. [The] Garrison was ordered under arms to protect the Duke, whom they intended to kill.§ Many of the Royals were shot before they could get their redress. I was Gunner on Waterport Guard. The Captain of the Guard came to me and ordered me to reverse guns that were pointing to the Spanish lines and point them on my comrade soldiers, who but a short time before had been fighting with me in Egypt. This was a horrid Christmas, for the night after Christmas, we were formed up against another Regiment* who broke out in rebellion, and killed many of them. I was at a gun that was formed up close in front of them and expected every man of us would have been put to death, our guns loaded and matches lighted. They frequently cried out 'Charge the Bugars,' 'Fire a volley at the Bugars.' I was more afraid than ever I was fighting against the French, and we found it more dangerous to fight against exasperated British soldiers standing out for their rights. They at last went off to their Barracks and all the regiments in the garrison surrounded them until daylight, when the Regiment was paraded and every 10th man picked out to be shot or transported. Eleven were actually transported, and a few days afterwards three were shot, and all the troops marched close past them. I could scarcely avoid stepping in their blood.

1803.

The Duke was obliged to fly to England.

Many times have I, while on this barren rock, lingered along the battlements of the fortress, to see the sun sinking behind some mountain

---

† 1st (or the Royal) Regiment of Foot (2nd battalion).

§ See *Life of H.R.H. Edward, Duke of Kent.* By the Rev. Erskine Neale. 1850. pp. 87-133.

* The 25th (or the Sussex) Regiment. William Dyott was Lieut.-Colonel of this regiment at the time, being then on leave in England. He records in his Diary—published in 1907 :—

"26 January, 1803. Received a letter to my utter astonishment from the Adjutant-General to say, that in consequence of what had happened at Gibraltar, I was by the Duke's (of York) order to join the regiment immediately. It seems there had been a spirit of mutiny [which] had shown itself in the garrison, in which the 25th took part."

The order was subsequently cancelled and he did not go out.

A GUNNER OF THE ROYAL REGIMENT OF ARTILLERY—1801.
From a MS. in the Royal Artillery Institution, Woolwich,
entitled,
Memorandum of Artillery Arrangements, etc., on the Expedition
to Egypt, 1801.
By Brig.-General Robert Lawson.
[Lawson was in command of the Royal Artillery of this force.]
This is the dress which Miller would have been wearing.

1803.

to the west, over my beloved country, never expecting to see it more; then would my eyes grow dim with tears, and my breast heave with sighs. I then would turn from the impressive landscape and fly to my companions to drown my sorrow in their wild and boisterous revelry.

1804.

On 8 October, 1804, I was promoted to Bombardier. The Plague was now raging in this garrison. Shocking to relate, I have seen 500 inhabitants carried out in the dead carts in one day, besides soldiers, which would sometimes amount to 100 of a day more. We had 5 hundred artillery in the garrison, out of which we lost upwards of 200 in six weeks. It was a dismal sight to see the dead carts prooling [? prowling] the streets and the Jews running away with their dead to prevent them being put into the cart among the Christians. We frequently threw 40 into one hole, clothes and all and some quite warm, and scarcely dead. Every person in the garrison had a shock of it more or less.

There was a strong party of soldiers every day ordered for digging holes and burying the dead, and frequently half of the party would be buried in the same holes they had themselves dug the day before. One of the artillery was ordered on this duty; he left his wife in bed well and hearty in the morning, but in the course of the day, as he was helping to bury a cart load of dead, he threw his own wife into the hole not taking notice till after she was thrown in, when he thought he knew her stockings, which were blue. He stood for a time quite struck, but recovering from his stupor he jumped into the hole to ascertain the truth, for the faces of those who died suddenly in the plague were much disfigured, and very bloody. He examined her hand and her two gold rings, which he took off. She left a large family.

[There is a gap here in the MS. of nearly 4 years.]

1808.

In August, 1808, on account of the French taking possession of Portugal and Spain, we were ordered to join the troops from England [which had] landed at Mondego Bay, and beat the French Army [in] two engagements, and entirely routed [them] and took them prisoners†

[Miller's Company arrived in the Tagus on 2 September, 1808, and was quartered in Fort St. Julian, about 10 miles due W. from Lisbon, on the N. bank of the river.]

I was now ordered to Lisbon and from thence, with an officer of Artillery, 1 Serjeant, 1 Corporal, 2 Bombardiers, and 30 Gunners, to join the 6th Regiment of foot, to proceed to Almeida§ and take possession of it, as the French refused to give it up to the Portuguese. This was a march of 300 miles for the first start.

As we were the first British troops that had marched through any of the towns, we were much caressed, and saluted with cries of ' Viva

---

† The battles of Roliça (17 August) and Vimieiro (21 August).
§ Almeida, a fortified town, in Portugal, five miles from the Spanish frontier, in the District of Guards, about 235 miles in direct line, N.E. from Lisbon.

1808. September.

Engles,' ' Bueno Englies,' ' Rumpu Francies,'‡ and in some of the large towns, of which we went through a great number, we were saluted with rockets, fires, and firing of fowling pieces, and the women covered us with flowers and laurel leaves; the ladies even threw laurel and flowers from the windows on us. At Coimbra we were obliged to give point to the front with our swords, to pass through the mob. They wanted to carry us on their backs. At a town called Larica I went and saw the Church where the French soldiers shot five friars at the altar. The blood was still to be seen, likewise the shot holes in the altar. To this town the French retreated after we had beat them and on a Market day, their Dragoons formed up in the Market Square, treading down men, women, children, and cattle.

We arrived in sight of Almeida on 1 October, 1808, after a long and tiresome march of 300 miles, and took up our abode in a Friar's Convent.

Next morning we were formed up at the gates of the fortress. The French marched out prisoners of war and we took possession of it. This fortress parts Portugal from Spain† and it is hard for a stranger to know whether the inhabitants are Portuguese or Spanish.

I remained two months in this place. I was next ordered to join a brigade* of guns which were going with the army to Spain. A soldier hung [hanged] for plunder.

Went in pursuit of the French army in Spain. First day's march, ran my sword through a mule that I could not get along. Very wet day.

Second day halted at [Ciudad] Rodrigo; remained there two days; from thence to Salamanca. Here I saw Stephen Pitcher, native of Melbury. I had not seen him for 13 years. The house where our ammunition was took fire; the drum beat to arms and all the artillery and 52nd Regiment went to secure it. Pitcher belonged to the 52nd, and hearing one of the artillery call Bombardier Miller, he went to the man and asked him if I came from Dorset, and being answered in the affirmative, he next day came and found me and had wine together.

I went and saw all the Churches, Colleges, Monasteries, Nunneries, of which are great numbers at this City. At the Gate entry of Salamanca, there hung the head of a man, and his quarters hung at four cross roads. He had been a Traitor.

From Salamanca we retreated back to Rodrigo, and from thence to Salamanca† again, and from thence we advanced to Benavente, from thence to Zamora, another fine large town. We still kept advancing until about 4 o'clock, Christmas Eve, when we were making ready to engage the enemy [on] Christmas Day. But our General hearing the enemy had got a reinforcement of 70,000 men [we] were obliged to retreat all night.

Christmas Day we passed through Palantua, in a most dreadful state, for it rained very hard for about a week. We made the best of our way,

‡ Literal translation—" Three cheers for the English," and " Damn the French."
* i.e. 6 guns, corresponding to the Field Battery of to-day.
† There is some confusion here as to places. ' Salamanca ' seems to be a mistake.

1808. December.

marching night and day, back to Benavente, and the enemy close at our heels. We saw 4 columns of French horse on a hill, as our army were passing in to the town. We drew up some of our guns and Infantry to oppose them, but they came no farther that day.

Two days afterwards they made their appearance in great force, and some of their Dragoons were crossing through the river (we had blown up the bridge) towards the town, but our Dragoons met and engaged them in the river, cut them to pieces and took a General prisoner.* The clashing of the swords were similar to a number of mowers whetting their scythes.

1809.

We were obliged to make the best of our way for Coruña, destroying all our baggage and stores by the way; even casks of dollars were rolled into the rivers. We passed through many fine towns, particularly La Baneza, Lugo, Astorga, Villafranca, Briganza [Betanzos.], &c., &c., but were too much exhausted by wet, cold, hunger, and want of rest to take much notice. We made a halt at Lugo [5-8 January], and offered the enemy battle [8 January], but they declined it, on account of their army not being up, as we thought. We drove them back 3 leagues and blew up a bridge, but they came after [us] again next day, occupying the same ground at night, as we left in the morning. They made prisoners of some of our men every day, that could not keep up, and scarcely a day passed but our rear guard made prisoners of some of the enemy's advance guard through venturing too far, after sharp skirmishes, and some of them dreadfully cut and wounded. I was several times in danger of being taken prisoner, for being very wet weather and the roads very bad with so many horses and carriages passing, it was dreadful travelling, and one half of the army without shoes. I got up to my knees in clay in the night coming into Lugo, and lost one of my shoes, and threw the other away, but I got a pair of ammunition shoes at Lugo, but too small. So I was obliged to wear them down at heel. So through bad shoes, and the old wound in my ankle getting troublesome with such a long forced march, it was generally midnight before I could come up to where the army halted, and many more as well as me.

Frosty weather now came in, which did not make it much better for us, for we were getting on the mountains where the snow frequently lay all the summer, which froze some of the men to death. Plague began among the Spanish Troops, but there was a very few of them with us.

One town that we passed through, we saw some Spanish soldiers carry some dead men into a yard. We looked in for curiosity and saw a large heap of dead bodies, froze together like lumps of dirt. Our officers soon ordered us away.

When we came to Villafranca, the Spaniards shut their houses on us, and we were ordered to break them open, (after all the Convents and Churches were full) and make our lodgings good for the night. Me and four more broke open a house where they had plenty of wood but they would not give us any. I went down stairs to take some, but they

* The action of 29 December, at Benavente, when General Lefebvre was taken prisoner.

1809.   January.

had some Spanish soldiers to guard it. They said one to the other kill him, and began to push me about. I asked them in Spanish, if that was the treatment they meant to give us after fighting for them. One of them very luckily pushed me against the stairs. I immediately ran up and told the four men to be on their guard or we should be all killed. One placed himself behind the door, and I and the other three stood with our swords drawn. In a few minutes after up came 3 Spanish soldiers with large staves and knives. The man behind the door ran one of them through, and I cut down another, and the third, had 3 swords on him. We left them all for dead. Soon after, we heard a great noise in pulling them away, and next morning at daylight when we marched away we saw a deal of blood on the stairs, which made us think they were all killed, which they very justly deserved. We made the door secure inside and kept all in, both the man of the house and his family. We then pulled down a partition that went across the room, and broke up the chairs and stools, to warm our selves. We saw some hams hung up, and a basket of eggs. We asked them to sell us some, and offered double the value, for we had nothing to eat all day, but they refused. But we took one ham, and as many eggs as we could eat, and fried it. We also saw a pig's skin full of wine in the room. We offered money for some, and the Spaniard finding that he might as well take the money as not, sold us as much as we chose to drink. We took care not to drink too much, for fear the Spaniards should take advantage of us. So I planted a sentry in the room while the rest slept, with orders to be alert in case of the Spaniards coming to waken us, for we could have killed an hundred of them coming up stairs, but we were not disturbed any more.

At this town we destroyed the remainder of wagons, stores, and ammunition, about 500 waggon loads, and even burned our knapsacks, so that we had only a few rounds of ammunition for each cannon left and it [required] more to protect us from the rascally, treacherous Spaniards than [from] our open enemy the French. So now we were light enough, our backs almost bare, our bellies empty, and no shoes to our feet. Our greatest burden was the Spanish lice; the few rags we had left were covered with them. We got our guns over the snowy mountains with great difficulty, and two days after we met fresh horses from Coruña which we had great need of, for we shot our horses as fast as they lost their shoes or got lame, that they may not fall into the hands of the enemy.

On our road to Coruña we burnt down a village because the people would not sell us anything.

At length [11 January] we arrived at Coruña and thought our hardships at an end. But, to our great surprise, there was only one British ship in the harbour, so that we were obliged to encamp on the heights, without tents, about 3 miles from the town.

Next day [12 January] I went into Coruña with a party to destroy all the guns, stores, magazines, and batteries belonging to the garrison that they should not fall into the hands of the enemy. There was also a party of horsemen sent to shoot all our horses, mules, and asses, which

1809. January.

[were] brought to a bank by the seaside so as to fall in the sea when shot.
The next day [13 January] I went with a party to destroy two large
magazines about five miles from Coruña: each magazine had 2,000
barrels of powder. During which time the French army came up and we
heard our picquets engaged with them. We had scarcely blown up the
magazines before the enemy Riflemen came on us and began to fire, but
we all made our escape and got safe to camp to the great surprise of our
army, who thought we were all taken prisoners, and General Moore was
heard to say those poor Artillerymen will all be killed or taken prisoners.

The enemy took up their position on the heights, about a mile and a
half from our line and began to erect batteries.

On 16 January, 1809, I was ordered out with the guns attached to
the ' Forlorn hope ' Picquets to keep the enemy's advance picquet at bay.
Our shipping had now come round from Vigo, where they had sailed to
from Coruña, having received intelligence that our army was retreating
to Vigo instead of Coruña, which proved very unfortunate, for had the
shipping been at Coruña on our arrival we should all have been safe on
board before the enemy would have been able to attack us, and we were
in a very poor state to wish for a battle, but, however bad our condition,
fight we must, or be driven into the sea, for the enemy, perceiving our
shipping were come and ready for us to embark, and that we were sending
off some of our guns and making preparations to embark, they sent out
strong parties to oppose our ' Forlorn hope ' picquet. We began to
fire on them thinking they were only going to relieve their night picquet,
but finding they advanced past their picquet, and [were] beginning to
fire, we began to think it a signal for [a] general action (or a " killing
day " as soldiers term it). Some sharp skirmishing took place between
the picquets and several men [were] killed and wounded; we drove them
back to their lines, and continued firing, until Generals Moore and Baird,
who were standing by the gun which I commanded, came and looked over
the wheel of the gun with a spy- glass, and said to me " don't fire any
more, Artillerymen, for I don't think it will come to a general engagement to-day." But he found to the contrary, for he was killed by a
French cannon ball that evening and General Baird's arm was shot off.

In the course of the day, having [had] nothing to eat, we sent six
men from the 3 guns belonging to the ' Forlorn hope ' picquet, to a
small village, Elvina, (which the Spanish peasants had been obliged to
leave) to seek for plunder. They had got some potatoes, a pan of butter,
and some fowls, but just as they were leaving the place, some French
Riflemen came down and fired on them. They were obliged to drop
their plunder and with difficulty got back to the guns. One man brought
about half a bushel of potatoes, which were boiling when the action took
place, and the shot came and knocked the kettle off the fire. We filled
our pockets with them half-boiled and ate them while fighting our guns.
The action began about 2 o'clock in the afternoon.* The enemy came
down in great fury, but our troops charged them so gallantly several

* A History of the Peninsular War, by Sir Charles Oman. 1902. Vol. I. p. 586. " But
between 1 30 and 2 o'clock, the French suddenly took the offensive."

VIEW OF THE BRITISH AND FRENCH POSITIONS BEFORE CORUNA, TAKEN FROM THE CITADEL.

From an illustration in ".A Narrative of the Campaign of the British Army in Spain, Commanded by His Excellency Lieut-General Sir John Moore, K.B.," by James Moore, 1809.

a b—British line.   c d —French line.   e—Magazine blown up on January 14, 1809.   f—The Village of Elvina.
g g—Heights occupied by the French on the morning of January 11.

1809. January.

times, even charged through their ranks, that they knew not what to make of us, and in place of driving us into the sea, as they expected, we fairly beat them back to their lines, and gained a complete victory, after a retreat of so many miles from Toro to Coruña, over an army five times our number, but with the loss of a great many brave men, who unfortunately lost their lives in such an unequal contest, after withstanding so many battles and hardships in the country, and were just on the point of leaving it.

During our skirmish with the enemy's picquet in the morning, two Spanish women very deliberately passed between us and the French while firing, as if regardless of their lives. They went about half a mile to a village, Elvina, that was deserted by the inhabitants, with the shot flying over them in all directions. In an hour after they returned by the same road and in the same manner, talking together. They would have stopped to see us fire, but we drove them away. We conjectured that the village they had visited was their late residence and [that they] had been to look for their property, which they would get but a poor account of after two armies plundering it in succession.

On the night of the 16th we got all our guns on board, and on the 17th the whole army made the best of their way and got on board, all in confusion. Not a single ship but had soldiers of every regiment in the army indiscriminately mixed.

The enemy came very soon after us close to the gates, but was obliged to retreat to a considerable distance, on account of two Companies of artillery,† who were sent to the garrison batteries, with the Spanish artillery that belonger to the place, opening their fire on them.

The enemy then brought several pieces of cannon to bear on the shipping, and [on] the troops in the boats, and fired on us as we embarked [and] cut some of the boats, loaded with soldiers, to pieces, and rendered some of the ships useless.

Having a fair wind [18 January] to blow us out of their reach we cut cables (as fast as the ships were nearly full of troops) and put to sea. Such a sight, I think, was never seen before—sometimes a dozen ships all entangled together, all in confusion, drifting before the wind, and soldiers climbing up their sides from the boats, and, had not the wind been fair to carry us out of reach of their guns, we must all have been lost. As we drifted down the harbour we saw hundreds of our soldiers, which had been doing duty in the garrison, sitting on the rocks by the water's side at the back of the town, waving their hats, and calling for boats to take them off and many women and children among them. They saw us pass without seeming to take any notice of them, and expecting every minute to be made prisoners, not knowing there were two Companies of Artillery left on the batteries which could keep the enemy out of the garrison for that night, and indeed not knowing that boats would be sent for them in the night.

† Captain Robert Truscott's and Captain Edward Wilmot's Companies of the 3rd Battalion, Royal Artillery—in 1928 designated 3rd Light Battery, R.A., and 13th Field Battery, R.A., respectively.

1809.   January.

But as soon as we were out of reach of the enemy we lay to, and after dark boats were sent to fetch off the two Companies of Artillery and all the stragglers they could find, which took up the whole night. The people that were on the rocks, what with cold, hunger, and fright at being left behind, were almost dead.

Next morning [18 January] we got under way, and bid farewell to Spain.

[To show how accurate Miller is in details and dates, the Despatch of Colonel John Harding, who was in command of the whole of the Artillery of Sir John Moore's army, is here given in full. It was addressed to the Deputy Adjutant-General, R.A., and is found in the Public Record Office—Letter Book, "From Officers, Foreign." W.O. 55/1194, pp. 183-9. It explains the part taken by the units of the Royal Artillery in the battle of Coruña and the concluding operations.

"Portsmouth. 29 January, 1809.

"SIR,

Having, in the course of my correspondence, detailed to you, for the information of the Master General [of the Ordnance], the march of the Royal Artillery through Spain, I have now to report that the Army took up a position before Coruña on the 11th, about five miles from town, and about the 14th they retired to a position nearer to the town by two miles.

Two Brigades of Artillery. Light 6 pounders were posted in this position by order of Sir John Moore, under the command of a Field Officer, and on the 15th four of the Light 6 pounders were removed for embarkation, by the Commander of the Forces' orders, and four Spanish 8 pounders advanced in their stead.

The following day, the 12th, I received the directions of Sir John Moore to commence and proceed with the embarkation of the Brigades of Artillery not employed in the advanced position. On the 13th the Commander of the Forces directed me to prepare to blow up a large magazine containing 12,000 barrels of British powder. I then represented to him that, from the communication I had now with the Spanish Artillery Officers, I did not think there was a sufficient quantity of powder in the magazines within Coruña (the fleet not having arrived), and proposed bringing in what I possibly could.

The 13th the Artillery were employed in bringing powder into the town of Coruña from the above-mentioned magazine, about four miles, and there being no road for carriages within a mile and a half of the magazine, the men were obliged to carry the barrels of powder that distance on their shoulders to the waggons; between two and three hundred barrels were conveyed into the town.

Having considered that the explosion of so much powder confined might destroy the town and injure the shipping, it took up the whole of the night of the 13th and great part of the day of the 14th, in opening 6,000 barrels of powder and spreading it on the ground round the magazine.

This magazine, together with another near it, containing about

1809. January.

300,000 British musquet cartridges and a great quantity of Spanish musquet cartridges, were blown up in a very masterly manner by Lieut.-Colonel Cookson on the 14th.

The 14th and 15th, the remainder of the Artillery that could be spared from the embarkation of the Brigades were employed in destroying the guns and mortars on the sea front and island within the bay; upwards of fifty heavy guns were dismounted, spiked, and shot wrapped round with canvas rammed down to the bottom of the cylinders; the carriages were also destroyed and thrown over the precipice, and with the assistance of one hundred Royal Marines on the evening of the 15th twenty heavy mortars were also dismounted and thrown over.

The Army was likewise supplied with ammunition on the 14th and 15th and completed to seventy rounds per man.

Having reported to the Commander of the Forces that there were 9,000 stand of British Arms in the Spanish Depôt, I proposed that the Army should be completed with Arms, and those that were not efficient should be changed, and in consequence of which near five thousand stand of new Arms were delivered to the Troops in lieu of Arms wanting or unserviceable.

On the 16th the enemy attacked our position, at which time Major Viney commanded the guns advanced in the position. Enclosed is a return of ordnance with the Officers, Non-Commissioned Officers, Gunners, Drivers and Horses attached to those guns.

As the action continued with great warmth, I considered it necessary to send up more ammunition, in addition to the four waggon loads of musquet ammunition placed close in the rear of the position, as approved by the Commander of the Forces. I therefore during the action procured from the Spanish magazines three waggons loaded with musquet and one waggon loaded with 8 pounder ammunition and forwarded them to the position. I likewise landed from the shipping a large proportion of light 6 pounder ammunition, but it was not required.

At night the Troops retired from the position into the town, and the guns were withdrawn at the same time. I had proposed, agreeable to a former arrangement with Sir John Moore, to embark them the following morning, from a sandy bay south-west of Coruña, but the weather would not permit it; the guns were spiked, the carriages destroyed, and the whole thrown over the precipice into deep water.

One Field Officer, (Major Beevor, commanding,) and three Companies of Artillery (a Return of whom are enclosed) remained on shore with the rear guard, by Sir John Moore's previous orders, to assist the Spaniards in manning the guns on the land front of Coruña, to keep possession of a small island in the bay, and to cover the embarkation of the troops from the citadel.

These Companies embarked with the rear guard in the night of the 17th and early in the morning of the 18th instant.

(Sd.)   J. Harding.

1809.   January.

RETURN OF CASUALTIES OF THE ROYAL ARTILLERY AND ROYAL ARTILLERY DRIVERS IN THE ACTION BEFORE CORUNA, JANUARY 16, 1809.

				MEN.		HORSES.	
				Killed.	Wounded.	Killed.	Wounded.
Royal Artillery	...	...	...	...	2	...	...
Royal Artillery drivers	...	...		2	...	2	...
Total	...	...	...	2	2	2	...

RETURN OF THE ROYAL ARTILLERY ATTACHED TO THE REAR GUARD OF THE ARMY ON THE EMBARKATION AT CORUNA, JANUARY 17 AND 18, 1809.

			Major.	Captains.	Subalterns	N.C.O.'s.	Gunners.	Total.
Total	...	...	1	5	3	36	253	298

Officers' Names.
Major R. Beevor—in command.
Captains—R. Thornhill, R. Truscott, and G. Bean.
2nd Captains—T. A. Brandreth and T. Greatley.
Lieutenants—W. E. Maling, F. Wright, and J. Darby.

RETURN OF THE ROYAL ARTILLERY AND ROYAL ARTILLERY DRIVERS IN THE ACTION BEFORE CORUNA, JANUARY 16, 1809.

	OFFICERS AND MEN.								ORDNANCE.				AMMUNITION.			
	Major.	Captains.	Subalterns.	Asst. Surgs.	N.C.O.'s.	Gunners.	Drivers.	Total.	Light 6 Pr.	Light 5½ in. Howitzer.	8 Pr. Spanish.	Total.	Light 6 Pr.	Light 5½ in. Howitzer.	8 Pr. Spanish.	Total.
R.A.	1	4	2	2	16	120	...	145	7	1	4	12	1,190	150	320	1,660
R.A. Drivers	...	...	2	...	8	...	84	94	...	...	...	...	...	...	...	...
Total	1	4	4	2	24	120	84	239	7	1	4	12	1,190	150	320	1,660

Waggons of Musquet Ammunition—Spare   ...   ...   4.

Officers, R.A.
Major J. Viney in command.
Captains R. Truscott and E. Wilmot.
2nd Captains T. Greatley and C. H. Godby.
Lieutenants J. Sinclair and T. N. King.
Assistant Surgeons F. P. Hutchesson and J. Price.

Officers, R.A. Drivers.
Lieutenant B. Abercrombie.
Lieutenant T. Reid.

]

1809. January.

Numbers of our men began to die on board the ships with the Spanish fever breaking out among us. But ·to our great joy on 27 January, 1809, we came in sight of England, the first sight of British land I had seen for near 14 years.

28. Passed through the Needles, and anchored at Spithead.

31. Went into Portsmouth harbour, where a great many troops (that had been no farther than Coruña) landed, but we were so ragged and lousy, that we were not permitted to land, but [had] to sail to the ports nearest to our different Quarters. Neither were our troubles to end here. We buried several men here, who died in the fever. Our Pay-Serjeant went on shore and brought us some slop shirts, shoes, stockings, &c., &c., which were soon as lousy as the old ones. We would frequently pull off our clothes and stamp on them with the heels of our shoes to kill the lice.

We now began to muster the men from the different ships, but our Company, that embarked at Gibraltar 110 strong, we could only muster 40 men, so that we lost 70 men out of one Company in 6 months.

On our first retreat in Spain [i.e. from Salamanca] the enemy got between us, so that part of our army went back to Portugal, and some of our Company went with that part that went to Portugal, about 10 [of whom] have since joined us.

We were again ordered out to Spithead, to try our fortunes once more, when the storms came on so frequent that we were several times nearly lost. Several ships were drove on shore and beat to pieces.

While we lay here, one of our men laid down his canteen with some rum in it. On going to get some rum out of it to make grog he found the cork out and the rum gone, and a monkey that belonged to the ship lying beside it drunk, and could not stand. He went to the Captain of the ship and told him if he did not make good the rum he would shoot the monkey, but the Captain would not comply. So the man loaded a pistol with peas and shot it.

We again got under way for the river Thames, but there came on such boisterous weather that the fleet was dispersed, and driven, some to every port in England. Our ship, with God's blessing, got safe to the Downs, and next morning put in at Ramsgate pier, where we immediately landed, and I once more got my foot on English ground. I could not help admiring the difference of the ruddy, and jolly appearance of the women and children, from the poor, thin, tawny creatures I had been so many years among, and the butchers' shops attracted my attention. But the sight was my share of all I saw for I had no money, and had 16 miles to march before I could get any, or anything to eat or drink, and a very bad march we had, for it rained the greatest part of the road. But we were well used to such fare, and knew it would soon be over, so we thought nothing of it.

At Spithead I was detached from the Company to another ship, with 10 Gunners, and on our arrival at the Downs we heard that the Company was lost on the passage, and when I got to Canterbury I went to the Officers of Artillery and asked for some money for myself and

1809.   February.

the 10 men that was with me. But they said they understood my Pay Serjeant and part of the Company were come to Canterbury that afternoon, but if I could not find him to come back and I should have as much as would carry us to Woolwich.

It was too late to find him that night, so I borrowed some money from a Serjeant until the morning. We drew our billets and went to them, and soon drowned all our hardships in brandy and beer, the first beer we had drank for many years. The landlord gave us a good supper, and a bed too good. I pulled off my shirt to avoid leaving any lice in the bed.

The next morning we fell in with the rest of the Company, who were glad to see us. They had heard that we were lost. I then began to make enquiry for the Pay-Master, and soon found him. Got £10 from him. Went and paid the Serjeant. Drank some porter and proceeded on the march for Woolwich.

On our arrival at Woolwich we were all taken to the hospital and inspected by the Surgeon, [who] ordered a warm bath and a basin of Caudle.§ Served with clothes and all our old clothes burnt before we went to the Barracks And, after we had our bellies full of porter we found ourselves quite comfortable.

Next day after I came to Woolwich I was promoted from Bombardier to Corporal.‡

22 February. I went with five more to Greenwich College to draw prize money for Egypt.

26. Left Woolwich for Canterbury, where we remained until 19 July, 1811. Our men began to die very fast in the Spanish fever.

In October, 1809, [probbly a mistake for 1810.] I went home on furlough. Dined with the Volunteers at Evershott, at the time of the Jubilee.* I left Melbury on my return from furlough, with 14 shillings in my pocket and had 200 miles to travel, and was obliged to sell my watch while on furlough. I marched the 200 miles in six days. I marched the last seventy miles on 1s. 6d. It was my first furlough and [I] was determined it should be my last.

1811.

On 13 June, 1811, I was married at St. Martin's Church, Canterbury, the first Church that Gospel was preached in in Great Britain.†

On 19 July, we were ordered from Canterbury to Hythe, Folkestone, Sandgate, Shorncliffe, Dymchurch, &c., &c., distributed on Coast commands. I was stationed at the Grand Tower (or Circular Redoubt). Here we had a fine view of Boulogne, and the French coast. It is near Dungeness light-house.

On this Command, we were frequently alarmed in the night and

‡ The actual date of his promotion was 1 February, 1809.

§ A warm drink consisting of thin gruel, mixed with wine or ale, sweetened and spiced, given chiefly to sick people : also to their visitors.—*The Oxford English Dictionary.*

* The 50th Anniversary of George III's accession to the throne, 25 October, 1810.

† He married Sarah Butcher. See Parish Register of St. Martin's Church, Canterbury.

obliged to get up and fire on French privateers which would come close under our guns.

On 1 October, 1811, I was promoted to Serjeant, and sent to Sandgate to act as Serjeant-Major.

1812.

On 18 February, our Company was ordered to Portsmouth and there to embark to join Lord Wellington in Spain, but before we marched, an order came from Woolwich to our Captain to send me to Head Quarters for the purpose of going on the Recruiting service. I tried very hard to get off from it, and to go with the Company, but to no purpose. I was obliged to go Recruiting. I therefore proceeded to Woolwich, receiving my beating order,* and instructions and went to Derby, where both myself and wife were laid up in the ague and fever for two months.

At Derby our son John was born, at half-past 11 o'clock [on] Wednesday morning, 6 May, 1812.

On 24 May, I was ordered to move with my party to Yeovil, in Somersetshire, where we arrived on 2 June, 1812, and remained at Yeovil until the Peace in 1814.

1813.

In July, 1813, I was laid up in a bad fever. In April, 1813, I marched six recruits to Woolwich.

Our daughter, Betty, was born at Yeovil on 11 October, 1813, at 3 o'clock in the morning. I lost upwards of 60 pounds while on the Recruiting Service.

1814.

On 23 April, 1814, I was ordered with my party to proceed for Woolwich. On settling my account, I was 40 pounds in the agent's debt, and got leave to work until I was clear.

On 31 December, 1814, I fell from a ladder down on a cart wheel, with an hundred-weight on my back. Cut my face, and fractured my skull.

1815.

I went to the hospital; the Doctors took 34 ounces of blood from me in two days, by bleeding both arms and cupping me three times in the forehead and twice in the back part of my head, which with the blood that I lost by the fall weakened me so that I could scarcely stand. It left such giddiness in my head that the Surgeon reported me unfit for service.

I was ordered before the Medical Board, and passed, and on 7 March, 1815, I passed the Ordnance General Board, before his Excellency the Lieutenant-General of the Ordnance, and on 19 March I obtained my discharge and pension, 1s. 6½d. per day, and bid adieu to soldiering.

THE END.

* A certificate granted by the War Office for recruiting purposes.

Printed in the United Kingdom
by Lightning Source UK Ltd.
123202UK00001B/139/A